ANIMAL ALBUMS
THE CAT FAMILY
BY GOLRIZ GOLKAR
eureka!
EUREKA!, AN IMPRINT OF BELLWETHER MEDIA BY FLUTTERBEE

Eureka! books turn real stories into unforgettable experiences. Clear, direct language and sharp, captivating imagery make it easy to follow your curiosity, one fascinating fact at a time.
Your Eureka! moment awaits!

This edition first published in 2026 by Bellwether Media, Inc.

For information regarding permission, write to Bellwether Media, Inc., Attention: Permissions Department, 3500 American Blvd W, Suite 150, Bloomington, MN 55431.

Library of Congress Cataloging-in-Publication Data is available at www.loc.gov or upon request from the publisher.

ISBN: 9798893048551 (hardcover)
ISBN: 9798893049558 (ebook)

Editor: Rebecca Sabelko Designer: Josh Brink Series Designer: Jeff Kollock

TABLE OF CONTENTS

WHAT ARE CATS?	4
THE HISTORY OF CATS	6
LIFE CYCLE	8
CAT LANGUAGE AND BEHAVIOR	10
CAT FAMILY TREE	12
CAT BIOGRAPHIES	14
CATS AND PEOPLE	42
GLOSSARY	46
WRITE ABOUT IT!	47
INDEX	48

WHAT ARE CATS?

Cats are mammals that belong to the *Felidae* family. There are at least 37 cat species in the world that are divided into two groups. Big cats include lions, tigers, jaguars, and leopards. Small cats include 29 other species, including domestic cats.

DOMESTIC CAT

CHEETAH

Cats are native to every continent except Antarctica and Australia. Domestic cats live near humans, but nearly all other types of cats live in the wild.

Cats are carnivores. All cats, except cheetahs, have retractable claws. Cats have different coat colors and patterns that are often based on their habitats.

RETRACTABLE CLAWS

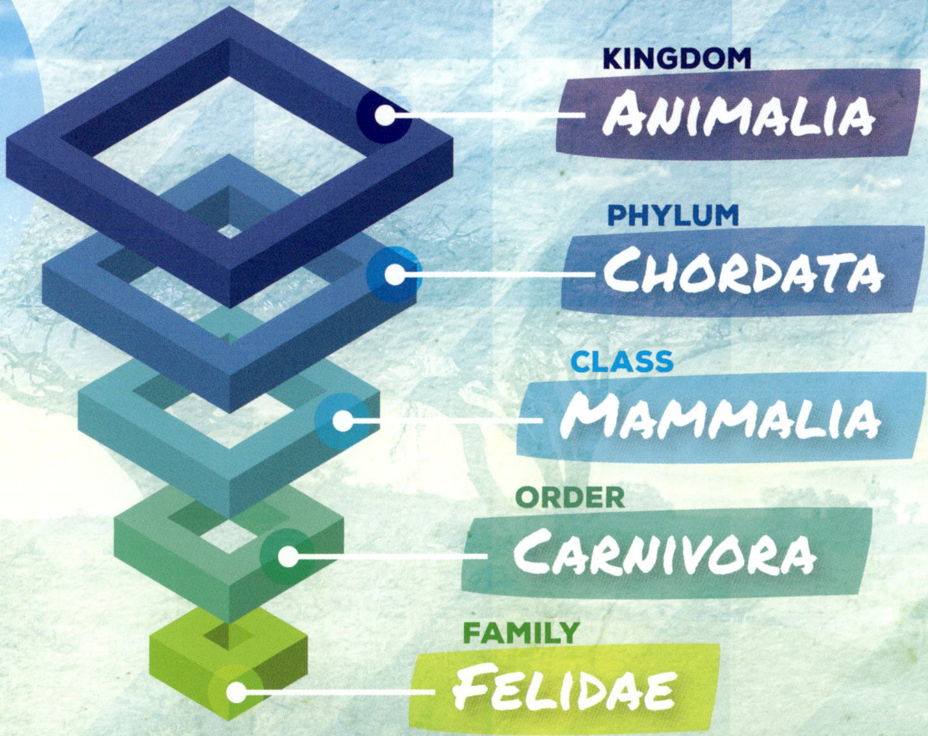
KINGDOM
ANIMALIA
PHYLUM
CHORDATA
CLASS
MAMMALIA
ORDER
CARNIVORA
FAMILY
FELIDAE

TAXONOMY CHART

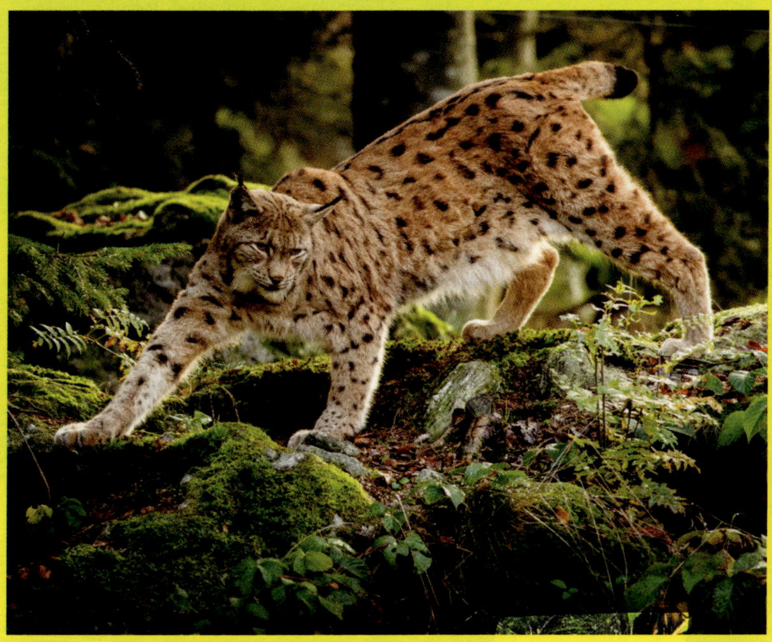

EURASIAN LYNX ▲

WILD CAT FACT

Some countries do not have wild cats. No wild cats are originally from Madagascar, Australia, New Zealand, or mainland Japan. They are not found on certain small islands or any polar regions.

NEW ZEALAND

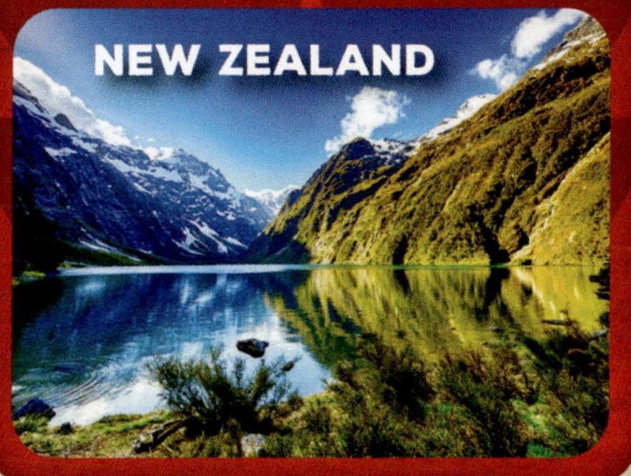

THE HISTORY OF CATS

FOSSIL

The oldest cat fossil dates to around 30 million years ago. Over millions of years, cats evolved and adapted. Most developed cone-shaped teeth, agility, and keen senses. As they moved into new habitats, their bodies changed to match where they lived. For example, cats in grassy areas developed solid, light-colored coats. Patterned fur became common on forest-dwelling cats. These changes helped them hide in their new homes.

Around 10,000 years ago, humans began farming. This attracted rodents, which then attracted cats. Cats became easier to tame as they lived near humans. Before long, domestic cats moved all over the world and new breeds developed.

EVOLUTIONARY EXCELLENCE

LIFE CYCLE

Most cats give birth to one to six kittens or cubs in a litter. Most species give birth once every one or two years. Domestic cats can give birth twice a year.

OCELOTS

Kittens and cubs are born unable to see or hear. Mothers give their babies milk and keep them safe. Kittens and cubs learn how to hunt while playing with their littermates. As they grow, they join their mothers on hunts.

JAGUAR CUB

Most male cats do not help raise their young. Young cats are often targeted by predators, including their fathers, during their first year of life.

AVERAGE LITTER SIZE

4 CUBS

3 KITTENS

3 CUBS

5 KITTENS

CAT LANGUAGE AND BEHAVIOR

SOUNDS

LION ROARING

Cats often hiss or growl when they feel threatened or to defend their territories. Lions, tigers, jaguars, and leopards roar to defend their territories and find mates. Smaller cats may purr when they are relaxed or to calm themselves. Domestic cats likely purr to communicate with humans.

Some cats meow to find one another. Domestic cats have many meowing sounds that help them communicate with humans.

BENGAL TIGERS
fighting over territory

SCENT MARKING

Cats mostly use scent to mark territories and show they are ready to mate. They may scratch or rub a surface or leave behind bodily fluids that tell other cats to behave a certain way.

CHEETAH ▲
scent marking a tree

CAT FAMILY TREE

BIG CATS

PANTHERINAE

▲ JAGUARS

LIONS ▲

An adult male lion's roar can be heard up to 5 miles (8 kilometers) away.

LEOPARDS ▲

▲ SNOW LEOPARDS

▲ CLOUDED LEOPARDS

TIGERS ▲

The oldest tiger fossils are about two million years old.

FELIDAE

SMALL CATS

FELINAE

▲ FISHING CATS

▲ OCELOTS
The left and right sides of an ocelot's coat do not have the same colors or patterns.

PUMAS ▲
Pumas can jump around 20 feet (6 meters) high.

▲ SERVALS

▲ LYNX

CHEETAHS ▲
A cheetah can run more than two times faster than the fastest human.

DOMESTIC CATS ▶

MORE THAN ▼
+20
OTHER SPECIES OF SMALL CATS

CAT BIOGRAPHIES

TIGERS

Tigers are the largest cats. There are six subspecies. They include the common Bengal, South China, Indochinese, Malayan, Sumatran, and Siberian.

APPEARANCE

Most tigers have yellow to orange fur. Every tiger has a unique pattern of black stripes. They have white bellies.

DIET

Tigers are apex predators that mostly hunt deer and wild pigs alone at night. They use sight and smell to stalk animals. Tigers ambush their prey and clasp their jaws onto an animal's neck.

WHERE DO THEY LIVE?

Tigers are found in parts of Russia, South Asia, Southeast Asia, and China. They live in swamps, grasslands, rainforests, and savannas.

WHITE TIGERS

White tigers are very rare in the wild. Most of the world's white tigers are bred by humans. Most often, two related tigers are needed to create the white color. This can cause health problems in white tigers.

FAMOUS TIGER

MACHLI

- **Location:** Ranthambore National Park in India
- **Life span:** 19 YEARS
- **Famous for:** A Bengal tiger that kept male tigers away from her territory. The loss of one eye and many teeth did not stop her from raising her cubs. She was believed to be the most photographed tiger in the world before her death in 2016.

SIZE COMPARISON

Siberian tiger	African lion	jaguar
933LBS (423 kg)	570LBS (259 kg)	350LBS (159 kg)

LIONS

Lions are the second-largest cats. The two subspecies are African lions and Asiatic lions. Lions live in groups called prides.

LION PRIDE

WHERE DO THEY LIVE?

Lions roam grasslands, savannas, forests, and scrublands. African lions live in sub-Saharan Africa. Asiatic lions live in the Gir Forest in northwestern India.

DIET

Lions are apex predators that stalk antelopes, zebras, and wildebeest at night. Females are the main hunters. Lions use their claws to drag prey to the ground. Then they bite its throat.

◀ ASIATIC LION

APPEARANCE

African lions have golden yellow to brown coats. Asiatic lions may have black, sandy, or gray coats. Males have large manes.

FAMOUS LION

SCARFACE

- **Location:** Masai Mara National Reserve in Kenya
- **Life span:** 14 YEARS
- **Famous for:** Scarface hurt his eye during a territorial fight, giving him a scar. He was featured on many science television programs and even had his own social media profile. He survived many fierce battles with other males.

LION PRIDES

Prides include several adult females, two to four adult males, and cubs.

▲ AFRICAN LION

SIZE COMPARISON

570LBS (259 kg)

African lion

220LBS (100 kg)

North American cougar

12LBS (5.4 kg)

Persian cat

CHEETAHS

Cheetahs are the fastest land mammal. They have semi-retractable claws that help them grip the ground as they run. There are five subspecies of cheetahs.

DIET

Cheetahs use their sharp vision to stalk prey. Then they sprint after the animal, trip it, and bite its throat. Cheetahs hunt antelopes, hares, and birds.

SIZE COMPARISON

220LBS (100 kg)

North American cougar

141LBS (64 kg)

South African cheetah

12LBS (5.4 kg)

Persian cat

WHERE DO THEY LIVE?

Most cheetahs live in Africa. Asiatic cheetahs live in Iran. They are found in grasslands, shrublands, savannas, and deserts.

FAMOUS CHEETAHS

TANO BORA, THE MAGNIFICENT FIVE

- **Location:** Masai Mara National Reserve in Kenya
- **Famous for:** For five years, five male cheetahs lived together. They hunted together and worked as a team. As of March 2025, only one of the cheetahs was alive. Scientists have learned that cheetahs are more capable of teamwork than they once thought.

APPEARANCE

Cheetahs have light brown coats with black spots. A black line runs from the inner corner of each eye down toward the mouth.

CHEETAH SPEED

A cheetah can go from 0 to 60 miles (97 kilometers) per hour in three seconds!

JAGUARS

Jaguars are the third largest of the big cats. They have the strongest bite!

WHERE DO THEY LIVE?

Jaguars live from northern Mexico to Argentina. Rainforests are their preferred habitats. They may also live in grasslands and savannas.

DIET

Jaguars are apex predators. They eat more than 85 species including capybaras, deer, fish, and caimans. These cats use excellent vision to stalk their prey. They ambush an animal and bite the back of its head.

SIZE COMPARISON

350LBS (159 kg)

jaguar

198LBS (90 kg)

African leopard

141LBS (64 kg)

South African cheetah

APPEARANCE

Jaguars have tan coats, but some are white, brown, or black. All have rose-shaped black spots called rosettes that help them hide as they hunt.

FAMOUS JAGUAR

EL JEFE
SPANISH FOR "THE BOSS"

- **Location:** Arizona and Mexico
- **Life span:** at least 12 YEARS
- **Famous for:** Jaguars once lived in the United States but were believed to be gone due to hunting and habitat loss. In 2011, the jaguar named El Jefe was first spotted in Arizona. He was last spotted in 2022.

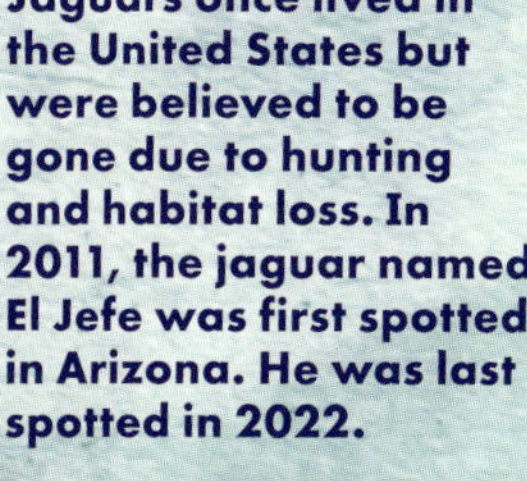

LEOPARDS

Leopards can leap 20 feet (6 meters) and jump up to 10 feet (3 meters) high! There are nine subspecies of leopards.

APPEARANCE

Most leopards have yellow to reddish-orange coats, but some are black. All leopards have rosette patterns, but the patterns are different for each subspecies.

VULNERABLE SPECIES

AMUR LEOPARD
CRITICALLY ENDANGERED

THREATS

hunting

habitat loss

loss of prey species

CONSERVATION EFFORTS

habitat protection

population monitoring

programs to stop hunting and illegal trade

WHERE DO THEY LIVE?

Leopards are found in the mountains, grasslands, deserts, and forests of Africa and Asia.

DIET

Leopards hunt at night. They use their sharp vision and hearing to stalk prey. They pounce on prey, then carry their kill high up into trees, stashing their meals where other animals cannot reach. Leopards eat many animals, including deer, antelope, fish, and birds.

LEOPARD OR NOT?

Snow leopards and clouded leopards are not true leopards. They are separate species with different traits.

SIZE COMPARISON

933LBS (423 kg)

Siberian tiger

220LBS (100 kg)

North American cougar

198LBS (90 kg)

African leopard

FISHING CATS

Fishing cats live near water and are uniquely adapted to catching fish. A double coat of fur keeps them warm in cold waters. There are two subspecies of fishing cats.

SIZE COMPARISON

141LBS (64 kg)

South African cheetah

31LBS (14 kg)

fishing cat

12LBS (5.4 kg)

Persian cat

VULNERABLE SPECIES

▼VULNERABLE▼

THREATS

- habitat loss and distances between habitats
- pollution
- hunting

CONSERVATION EFFORTS

protection under wildlife protection programs and wetland protection programs

APPEARANCE

Fishing cats have long heads and stocky bodies. Their grayish-brown fur has black spots and stripes.

DIET

Fishing cats hunt in shallow waters. They scoop up prey with their paws or grab animals with their teeth. They mostly eat fish.

WHERE DO THEY LIVE?

Fishing cats live in the marshes, jungles, swamps, and mangroves of South Asia and Southeast Asia.

OCELOTS

Ocelots are quite diverse depending on where they live. Scientists recognize two subspecies, but they have a lot to learn about these small cats.

APPEARANCE

Ocelots have golden or gray coats and white bellies. Black stripes, spots, and rosettes cover their bodies. They have large paws and long tails.

OCELOT PAW

SOUTH AMERICAN OCELOT

NORTH AMERICAN OCELOT

SIZE COMPARISON

198LBS (90 kg)

African leopard

35LBS (16 kg)

ocelot

12LBS (5.4 kg)

Persian cat

DIET

Ocelots use sight, hearing, and smell to stalk rodents, reptiles, and small mammals at night. Adapted ankle joints help them climb trees easily to hunt birds. They also swim to catch fish.

RAINFOREST

WHERE DO THEY LIVE?

Ocelots are found in Mexico and Central and South America. Small populations live in Texas and possibly Arizona. They are found in rainforests, grasslands, and brushlands.

VULNERABLE SPECIES

LEOPARDUS PARDALIS ALBESCENS

ENDANGERED

THREATS

CONSERVATION EFFORTS

restoring habitats

data collection of ocelots in Texas and northeastern Mexico

CARACALS

Caracals are known for their large, black-tufted ears. Subspecies have been recognized in the past, but there are no recent studies on different types.

BLACK-TUFTED EARS

APPEARANCE

Caracals have golden or reddish coats. Their chins, throats, and bellies are white. They have black markings around their eyes and black fur near their whiskers.

VULNERABLE SPECIES

MOST SUBSPECIES OUTSIDE SUB-SAHARAN AFRICA NEAR THREATENED TO CRITICALLY ENDANGERED

THREATS

hunting

habitat loss

poisoning

getting hit by vehicles

illegal trade

CONSERVATION EFFORTS

protection programs in parts of their range

efforts to learn about caracal status

WHERE DO THEY LIVE?

Caracals live in dry climates. They are found in mountains, savannas, and woodlands in Africa, the Middle East, and Asia.

HOW HIGH?

Caracals can jump as high as 10 feet (3 meters) in the air!

DIET

These cats hunt at night. Furry footpads help them silently stalk prey before they attack. Caracals often hide their kill in trees to eat later. They commonly eat rodents, mongooses, monkeys, and birds.

SIZE COMPARISON

141LBS (64 kg)

South African cheetah

80LBS (36 kg)

Eurasian lynx

44LBS (20 kg)

caracal

KODKODS

Kodkods are the smallest wild cats in the Americas. They are also called *guiñas* or Chilean cats. There are two subspecies.

KODKOD
Range in the Wild

= Range

WHERE DO THEY LIVE?

Kodkods only live in Chile and Argentina. They prefer forests with dense shrubs located near streams and coastal areas.

CHILEAN FOREST

DIET

Kodkods stalk prey both day and night. They mostly hunt lizards, rodents, birds, and rabbits. They also eat chickens and dead animals.

ARGENTINEAN FOREST

SIZE COMPARISON

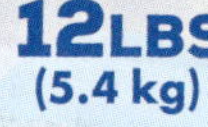

220LBS (100 kg)	12LBS (5.4 kg)	6.6LBS (3 kg)
North American cougar	Persian cat	kodkod

APPEARANCE

Kodkods have beige, reddish brown, or gray-brown coats with black spots. Black stripes mark their short, thick tails. Their faces have black stripes, and their ears are small and rounded.

FAMOUS KODKOD

PIKUMCHE

- **Location:** Fauna Andina reserve, Chile
- **Date of birth:** 2017
- **Famous for:** Pikumche was only 10 days old when a predator killed his mother. He has been raised by workers at a reserve. Pikumche is so used to human care that he cannot be released back into the wild.

PUMAS

Pumas have the largest range of any land mammal in the western hemisphere. Different subspecies have been described. Recent studies suggest there may be two.

WHERE DO THEY LIVE?

Pumas are found in swamps, deserts, forests, and chaparrals throughout the Americas.

DIET

Pumas stalk large prey at dawn and dusk. They jump on prey and deliver a deadly bite to the back of the neck. They eat deer, moose, coyotes, squirrels, and raccoons.

APPEARANCE

Most pumas have grayish brown to reddish brown coats with long, black-tipped tails. Their colors vary by region and season. Their hind legs are larger and stronger than their front legs.

FAMOUS PUMA

P-22 OR "HOLLYWOOD CAT"

- **Location:** Griffith Park in Los Angeles, California
- **First sighting:** 2012
- **Famous for:** P-22 was recorded living near the Hollywood sign in Los Angeles, California, for more than 10 years. His range was the smallest ever recorded.

CAT OF MANY NAMES

Pumas hold an official world record for the mammal with the most names at more than 40! Some of their names are cougars, mountain lions, panthers, and catamounts.

SIZE COMPARISON

933 LBS (423 kg)

Siberian tiger

220 LBS (100 kg)

North American cougar

198 LBS (90 kg)

African leopard

SAND CATS

Sand cats are tiny wild cats that can handle extreme temperature changes. The most recent studies show there are likely two subspecies.

APPEARANCE

Sand cats have grayish brown to beige coats and striped tails. Their furry foot pads protect them from extreme temperatures and help them move on sand.

DISTANT TRAVELERS

Scientists think some sand cats have huge home ranges. They travel so far that scientists have trouble tracking them.

SIZE COMPARISON

933LBS (423 kg)

Siberian tiger

80LBS (36 kg)

Eurasian lynx

7.5LBS (3.4 kg)

sand cat

DIET

Sand cats hunt by listening for underground prey. They dig for the animal, then take deadly bites. Rodents are their main prey. They also eat birds, spiders, and reptiles. Sometimes they attack venomous snakes.

WHERE DO THEY LIVE?

Sand cats are found from the Sahara Desert in Africa, throughout the Arabian Peninsula, to areas of central Asia. They live in sandy deserts and rocky valleys.

VULNERABLE SPECIES

FELIS MARGARITA THINOBIA

NEAR THREATENED TO CRITICALLY ENDANGERED

THREATS

hunting

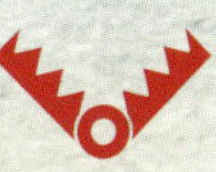
trapping

introduction of feral and domestic cats that compete for food and spread diseases

habitat loss

CONSERVATION EFFORTS

protection against hunting in parts of their range

JUNGLE CATS

Jungle cats are closely related to domestic cats. The most recent studies suggest there are likely three subspecies.

DIET

Jungle cats stalk prey. They often grab prey with their mouths. They eat rodents, fish, reptiles, birds, and insects.

VULNERABLE SPECIES

FELIS CHAUS FULVIDINA

THREATENED TO ENDANGERED

THREATS

- hunting
- trapping
- poisoning
- pollution
- habitat loss

CONSERVATION EFFORTS

protection against hunting in parts of their range

SIZE COMPARISON

APPEARANCE

Jungle cats have light brown or reddish coats and have stripes across their legs. Their large round ears have tufts.

WHERE DO THEY LIVE?

Jungle cats are found in Africa, Asia, and the Middle East. Despite their name, they do not usually live in jungles. They are sometimes called swamp cats or reed cats because they prefer reed beds, thick brush, and swamps.

LYNX

There are four species of lynx, including Iberian lynx, Eurasian lynx, Canada lynx, and bobcats.

APPEARANCE

Lynx have red, brown, or gray coats with dark spots. They have black ear tufts and short tails.

BOBCAT

CANADA LYNX

SIZE COMPARISON

141LBS (64 kg)

South African cheetah

80LBS (37 kg)

Eurasian lynx

12LBS (5.4 kg)

Persian cat

DIET

Lynx mostly stalk prey before they grab it with their front claws. They take down prey by biting its neck. Most lynx eat rabbits, rodents, and deer.

PREDATORS AND PREY

Canada lynx mainly eat snowshoe hare. When snowshoe hare populations rise or drop, Canada lynx populations do as well.

WHERE DO THEY LIVE?

Lynx live in forests across the northern hemisphere. Eurasian lynx are found in Europe and Asia. Iberian lynx live in the Iberian Peninsula in Spain. Canada lynx and bobcats are found in North America.

VULNERABLE SPECIES

IBERIAN LYNX
VULNERABLE

THREATS

- hunting
- habitat loss
- loss of prey
- disease

CONSERVATION EFFORTS

- restoring habitats
- reintroduction into the wild
- breeding programs

DOMESTIC CATS

Domestic cats are a group of over 70 breeds. They have different sizes, colors, and features.

◀ MAINE COON

= Origin

WHERE DO THEY LIVE?

Domestic cats live on every continent except Antarctica. House cats stay mostly near their homes. Stray and feral cats may wander long distances but stay close to human settlements.

DIET

House cats usually eat food provided by humans. Feral and stray cats hunt rodents, birds, and fish.

APPEARANCE

Domestic cats can have many different colors of fur. They may be spotted or striped. Their fur can be short or long. Some have wavy or curly fur. A few breeds are hairless. Most have long tails.

FAMOUS DOMESTIC CAT

TARDAR SAUCE, ALSO CALLED GRUMPY CAT

- **Location:** Arizona
- **Lifespan:** 2012 to 2019
- **Famous for:** Tardar Sauce was a domestic shorthair cat with an unusually grumpy-looking face. She was nicknamed Grumpy Cat. Her constant frown made her popular on the internet. Her face was featured in art, advertising, and books.

PET CATS

In 2024, more than 42 million households in the U.S. had a domestic cat as a pet.

SIZE COMPARISON

22LBS (10 kg) Maine coon cat

12LBS (5.4 kg) Persian cat

8LBS (3.6 kg) Singapura cat

CATS AND PEOPLE

Cats have been important to humans for thousands of years. Ancient domestic cats helped people get rid of pests while serving as pets. Many people around the world honored cats in their art. Today, different cat species are featured in books, art, film, and advertising.

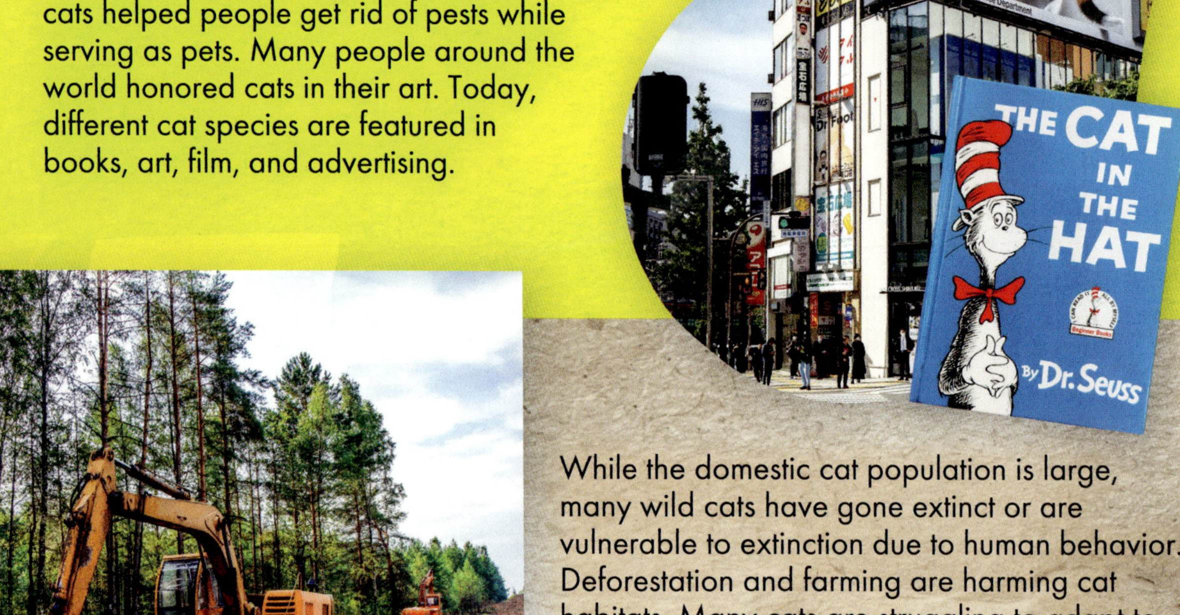

DEFORESTATION

While the domestic cat population is large, many wild cats have gone extinct or are vulnerable to extinction due to human behavior. Deforestation and farming are harming cat habitats. Many cats are struggling to adapt to habitat changes caused by climate change. Another major threat is illegal hunting and wildlife trading.

FOLKLORE PROFILE

NAME:

BASTET

COUNTRY:

EGYPT

FAMOUS FOR:

Bastet is the Egyptian goddess of cats, the home, and childbirth. The goddess protects the home from illness and evil spirits, especially watching over women and children. She has the head of a cat and the body of a woman.

Many organizations are working to protect cats. Some organizations put stray domestic cats up for adoption. Domestic cats are often sterilized to control their population and prevent diseases.

Other organizations work to protect wild cats. People work to pass laws that make sure habitats are not harmed. Educational programs teach farmers methods to live alongside cats instead of hunting them. Some programs work to stop illegal hunting and wildlife trading.

One of the biggest ways humans can help wild cats is by encouraging governments to pass laws that fight climate change. By helping wild cat species, Earth will be a healthier place!

GLOSSARY

adapted—changed over a period of time

advertising—the act of announcing or promoting something to get people to buy it or use it

agility—the ability to move with quick, easy grace

ambush—to attack from a hiding place

apex predators—animals at the top of the food chain that are not preyed upon by other animals

breeds—types of domestic cats

carnivores—animals that only eat meat

chaparrals—areas of land covered in shrubs that have dry summers and wet winters

climate change—a human-caused process in which Earth's average weather changes over a long period of time

deforestation—the act of cutting down a wide area of trees

diverse—made up of animals that are different from one another

domestic—related to living near or around human settlements

evolved—changed from one form into a new form

extinct—no longer living

feral—related to cats that have escaped from domestication and become wild

habitats—natural homes of plants and animals

hemisphere—a half of the earth

mammals—warm-blooded animals that have backbones and feed their young milk

mangroves—groups of trees and shrubs that grow along coastlines

marshes—wetlands filled with grasses and other plants with stems

peninsula—a section of land that sticks out from a larger piece of land and is almost completely surrounded by water

rainforests—thick, green forests that receive a lot of rain

retractable—able to be pulled back in

scrublands—dry lands that have mostly low plants and few trees

species—groups of living things that are alike and can reproduce with one another; subspecies are particular types of animals that exist within a species.

stalk—to hunt slowly and quietly

sterilized—prevented the ability to reproduce

vulnerable—at risk of becoming endangered

WRITE ABOUT IT!

- What species of cat would you like to learn more about? **Why?**

- What cat behavior do you think is the most interesting? **Why?**

- **What** changes can you make in your life that could help keep cats and their habitats safe?

INDEX

Bastet, 43
caracals, 28–29
cheetahs, 4, 9, 13, 18–19
domestic cats, 4, 6, 8, 9, 10, 13, 36, 40–41, 42, 44
El Jefe, 21
evolutionary excellence, 7
fishing cats, 13, 24–25
jaguars, 4, 10, 12, 20–21
jungle cats, 36–37
kodkods, 30–31
leopards, 4, 10, 12, 22–23
lions, 4, 9, 10, 12, 16–17
lynx, 9, 13, 38–39
Machli, 15
ocelots, 13, 26–27
P-22, 33
Pikumche, 31
pumas, 13, 32–33
sand cats, 34–35
Scarface, 17
Tano Bora, 19
Tardar Sauce, 41
taxonomy chart, 5
tigers, 4, 10, 12, 14–15
vulnerable species, 22, 24, 27, 28, 35, 36, 39, 42

The images in this book are reproduced through the courtesy of: stuporter, front cover (caracal); christian vinces, front cover (jaguar), pp. 12 (jaguars), 20 (top); visa, front cover (tiger); Ekaterina Kolomeets, front cover (cat); Eric Isselée, front cover (lion), pp. 3 (tiger), 4 (tiger stripes), p. 14 (appearance), 22-23 (appearance), 41 (appearance); Akarawut, front cover (moss); Tri Visuals, front cover (plant); fantom_rd, p. 3 (top); Grispb, pp. 2-3 (African savannah), 9 (African savannah), 12-13 (African savannah); olegkruglyak3, pp. 2-3 (blue sky), 6 (blue sky), 10-11 (blue sky), 14-15 (blue sky), 42-43 (blue sky); belyaaa, pp. 4-5 (cat); Brian, p. 4 (cheetah); Michael Cola, p. 4 (puma); byrdyak, p. 4 (lion skin); piyagoon, p. 4 (jaguar rosettes); yvsedova, p. 4 (lynx spots); JAKLZDENEK, p. 5 (Eurasian lynx); Fyle, p. 5 (New Zealand); Mardoz, p. 6 (fossil); New Africa, p. 6 (cat breeds); Szike, p. 6 (cat & prey); picture.jacker, p. 7 (jaguar); Jon Anders Wiken, p. 7 (lynx ears); Fiona Ayerst, p. 7 (claws); Leca Isabelle, p. 7 (teeth); slowmotiongli, pp. 8 (ocelots), 12 (tigers), 13 (fishing cats), 25, 28 (bottom left), 34 (top), 35 (bottom left), 36 (top); Esin Deniz, p. 8 (cats); Eric Isselee, pp. 8 (jaguar cub), 17 (appearance), 33 (appearance); outdoorsman, p. 9 (pumas); Nick Dale, p. 9 (cheetah); kcapaldo, p. 9 (Canada lynx); Lori Labrecque, p. 9 (African lion); Moomusician, p. 9 (Ragdoll cat); SteffenTravel, p. 10 (lion); Dhritiman, p. 10 (Bengal tigers); DimaBerlin, p. 11 (cat scent); geoffkuchera, p. 11 (bobcat scent); blove, p. 11 (cat scratch); Dr Ajay Kumar Singh, p. 11 (cheetah scent marking); EcoView, p. 12 (lions); Brian Stuart Nel, p. 12 (leopards); evelinawarendh, p. 12 (snow leopards); B.Allen, p. 12 (clouded leopards); elitravo, p. 13 (ocelots); Evgeniyqw, p. 13 (pumas); photogallet, p. 13 (servals); Vaclav Matous, p. 13 (lynx); MD.AL-AMIN_KHAN, p. 13 (cheetahs); Konstantin Zaykov, p. 13 (domestic cats); julianwphoto, p. 14 (top); GUDKOV ANDREY, p. 14 (bottom left); Sourabh, p. 14 (bottom right); ondrejprosicky, p. 15 (Siberian tiger); Bhavik Thaker/ Wikimedia, p. 15 (Machli); Simon Dannhauer, pp. 16-17 (Tanzania, Africa); Lennjo, p. 16 (lion pride); Stu Porter, pp. 16 (bottom right), 18 (diet bottom middle); Dekajhon, p. 16 (Bottom left); Mariola Anna S, p. 17 (Asiatic lion); Adogslifephoto, p. 17 (scarface); Maciej Czekajewski, pp. 18-19 (Kenya); AB Photo Master, p. 18 (top); Ahmed Abubasel, p. 18 (diet top middle); PACO COMO, pp. 18-19 (appearance); Pranav Chadha, p. 19; ruek66, p. 19 (Tano Bora); THP Creative, pp. 20-21 (Mexico Jungle); michaklootwijk, p. 20 (capybara); Tomas, p. 20 (caiman); FotoRequest, p. 20 (bottom left); anankkml, pp. 21 (appearance), 28-29 (appearance); Sarah Cheriton-Jones, p. 21 (rosettes); U.S. Fish and Wildlife Service/ Wikimedia, p. 21 (El Jeff); Adrian Dockerty, p. 21 (bottom); Image'in, pp. 22-23 (African savannah); milkovasa, p. 22 (top); ShutterSparrow, p. 22 (Amur Leopard); bono, pp. 22-23 (bottom middle); Artem Avetisyan, p. 23; Richard Whitcombe, pp. 24-25 (mangrove forests); PhotocechCZ, p. 24; photocech, p. 24 (bottom left); Andreas Ruhz, p. 24 (bottom right); Vladimir Wrangel, p. 25 (appearance); Vladimir Kazakov, p. 25 (mangrove); Imago Photo, pp. 26-27 (amazon rainforest); Andrea Izzotti, p. 26 (ocelot paw); Hans Wagemaker, p. 26 (South American ocelot); Chris Rogers/ Getty Images, p. 26 (North American ocelot); McDonald Wildlife Photography Inc./ Getty Images, p. 27 (top); gustavofrazao, p. 27 (rainforest); staoist520, p. 27 (bottom left); Pix By Marti, p. 27 (bottom right); HandmadePictures, pp. 28-29 (National Park, Zimbabwe); rebius, p. 28 (top); Jenhung Huang, pp. 28-29 (bottom right); Martin Harvey/ Getty Images, p. 29 (top); Gerard Lacz, p. 29 (bottom); saiko3p, pp. 30-31 (Nahuel Huapi National Park), 30 (Argentinean forest); Jim Sanderson/ Wikimedia, p. 30 (top); Asura senpai, p. 30 (Chilean forest); Joel Sartore/ Photo Ark/ Minden, pp. 30, 30-31 (appearance), 31; AlexDreamliner, pp. 32-3 (marsh edge); Carol, p. 32 (top); Gerald Peplow, p. 32 (chaparral); Mari_art, p. 32 (bottom left); KenCanning, p. 32 (bottom right); Agami Photo Agency, p. 33 (top); National Park Service/ Wikimedia, p. 33 (P-22); Blar Studio, pp. 34-35 (United Arab Emirates); Anastassiya, p. 34 (appearance); MikeLane45, p. 34; Animals Animals/ SuperStock, p. 35; cceliaphoto, p. 35 (Sahara Desert); Cloudtail, p. 35 (bottom right); Lizavetta, pp. 36-37 (Nile river); imageBROKER.com GmbH & Co. KG/ Alamy Stock Photo, p. 36 (middle); Petra Karstedt/ Wilfried Berns/ Wikimedia, p. 36 (bottom left); Tomal Das/ Getty Images p. 36 (bottom right); RealityImages, pp. 36-37; Chintan Mehta, p. 37 (middle); Jose Luis Stephens, pp. 38-39 (Mount Rainier); Scott E Read, p. 38 (bobcat); Danita Delimont, p. 38 (Canada lynx); Ondrej Prosicky, p. 38 (Eurasian lynx); Staffan Widstrand, p. 39 (top); BlueBarronPhoto, p. 39 (snowshoe hare); JoseAngel, p. 39 (bottom left); Jesus Cobaleda, p. 39 (bottom right); jovannig, pp. 40-41 (central park New York); seregraff, p. 40 (top left); s8, p. 40 (top right); Romuald, p. 40 (middle); Mouse family, p. 40 (bottom); Asichka, p. 41 (top left); andreshka, p. 41 (top right); Bruce Glikas/ Contributor/ Getty Images, p. 41 (Tarder Sauce); 9Air, p. 42 (top); ZikG, p. 42 (book); Maksim Safaniuk, p. 42 (deforestation); Artacke Pictures, p. 42 (bottom); AllieGraphix, p. 42 (bottom left); Jerni, p. 43; Anonymous/ Public Domain/ Wikimedia, p. 43 (Bastet); Cloudcounter/ Wikimedia, p. 43 (flag); Shwe Paw Mya Tin/ AP Newsroom, p. 44 (top); NurPhoto/ Contributor/ Getty Images, p. 44 (middle); San Francisco Chronicle/ Hearst Newspapers/ Contributor/ Getty Images, p. 44 (bottom left); Anna, p. 44 (bottom right) Foto24/ Contributor/ Getty Images, p. 45 (top); Damian Lugowski, p. 45 (middle); Dzha, p. 45 (bottom left); Ana Vasileva, p. 45 (bottom right).